EMMANUEL JOSEPH

Financial Odyssey, Navigating the Complexities of International Markets and Investments

Copyright © 2025 by Emmanuel Joseph

All rights reserved. No part of this publication may be reproduced, stored or transmitted in any form or by any means, electronic, mechanical, photocopying, recording, scanning, or otherwise without written permission from the publisher. It is illegal to copy this book, post it to a website, or distribute it by any other means without permission.

First edition

This book was professionally typeset on Reedsy.
Find out more at reedsy.com

# Contents

| | | |
|---|---|---|
| 1 | Chapter 1: The Foundation of International Markets | 1 |
| 2 | Chapter 2: The Role of Central Banks in Global Finance | 3 |
| 3 | Chapter 3: The Impact of Geopolitical Events on Markets | 5 |
| 4 | Chapter 4: Understanding Exchange Rates and Currency Markets | 7 |
| 5 | Chapter 5: The Role of Multinational Corporations | 9 |
| 6 | Chapter 6: The Importance of Diversification in Investment | 11 |
| 7 | Chapter 7: Risk Management in International Investments | 13 |
| 8 | Chapter 8: The Role of Technology in Global Finance | 15 |
| 9 | Chapter 9: The Influence of Global Trade Agreements | 17 |
| 10 | Chapter 10: The Future of International Markets | 19 |
| 11 | Chapter 11: Emerging Markets and Investment Opportunities | 21 |
| 12 | Chapter 12: Strategies for Successful International... | 23 |
| 13 | Chapter 13: The Role of Ethical and Sustainable Investing | 25 |
| 14 | Chapter 14: The Role of Financial Institutions in Global... | 27 |
| 15 | Chapter 15: The Path Forward for Global Investors | 29 |

# 1

# Chapter 1: The Foundation of International Markets

Navigating the realm of international markets begins with understanding the foundation upon which these markets are built. At their core, international markets are an intricate web of economic activities and exchanges that connect different countries and regions. Key elements such as foreign exchange, global trade agreements, and cross-border investments come into play, influencing how goods, services, and capital flow across borders. The dynamics of international markets are governed by a myriad of factors including geopolitical events, regulatory policies, and economic indicators.

To gain a solid footing in international markets, it is essential to comprehend the significance of currency exchange rates. The fluctuating value of currencies affects everything from the cost of imports and exports to the profitability of multinational corporations. Factors such as interest rates, inflation, and political stability play a crucial role in determining exchange rates, making them a pivotal aspect of international market analysis. Additionally, the role of central banks and their monetary policies cannot be overlooked as they strive to maintain economic stability and control inflation.

Another cornerstone of international markets is global trade. Trade agreements such as the North American Free Trade Agreement (NAFTA) and the Trans-Pacific Partnership (TPP) have reshaped the landscape of international trade by reducing tariffs and fostering cooperation among member countries. These agreements create opportunities for businesses to expand their reach, access new markets, and benefit from economies of scale. However, they also introduce complexities such as compliance with diverse regulations and navigating trade disputes.

Finally, international markets are characterized by the movement of capital across borders. Foreign direct investment (FDI) and portfolio investments are two primary forms of cross-border capital flows. FDI involves establishing or acquiring businesses in foreign countries, contributing to economic growth and job creation. On the other hand, portfolio investments involve the purchase of financial assets such as stocks and bonds in foreign markets. Both forms of investment come with their own set of risks and rewards, requiring investors to conduct thorough due diligence and risk assessment.

# 2

# Chapter 2: The Role of Central Banks in Global Finance

Central banks play a pivotal role in shaping the landscape of global finance. Their primary responsibility is to implement monetary policy, which involves managing the money supply and interest rates to achieve macroeconomic objectives such as price stability, full employment, and economic growth. By influencing the cost and availability of money, central banks can impact consumer spending, business investment, and overall economic activity.

One of the key tools at the disposal of central banks is the setting of interest rates. Lowering interest rates can stimulate economic activity by making borrowing cheaper for consumers and businesses, thereby encouraging spending and investment. Conversely, raising interest rates can help curb inflation by reducing the demand for credit and slowing down economic activity. The decisions made by central banks regarding interest rates have far-reaching implications for global financial markets, affecting currency values, stock prices, and bond yields.

In addition to interest rate policy, central banks also engage in open market operations, which involve the buying and selling of government securities to regulate the money supply. By purchasing securities, central banks inject liquidity into the financial system, increasing the amount of money available for lending and spending. Conversely, selling securities withdraws liquidity, tightening the money supply. These operations are crucial for maintaining financial stability and preventing excessive inflation or deflation.

Another important function of central banks is acting as lenders of last resort. During times of financial distress or economic downturns, central banks provide emergency funding to financial institutions facing liquidity crises. This support helps prevent bank failures and systemic risks that could lead to broader financial instability. The actions taken by central banks during crises, such as the global financial crisis of 2008, underscore their critical role in maintaining the stability of the financial system.

3

# Chapter 3: The Impact of Geopolitical Events on Markets

Geopolitical events have a profound impact on international markets, often causing significant fluctuations in asset prices and investor sentiment. These events can range from political elections and government policies to conflicts and natural disasters. Understanding the potential effects of geopolitical events on markets is essential for investors seeking to navigate the complexities of global finance.

Political elections, for instance, can create uncertainty and volatility in financial markets. Changes in government leadership or shifts in policy direction can lead to fluctuations in currency values, stock prices, and bond yields. Investors closely monitor election outcomes to assess the potential implications for trade policies, regulatory frameworks, and fiscal measures. For example, a government that adopts protectionist policies may trigger concerns about trade barriers and tariffs, impacting global trade and investment flows.

Geopolitical conflicts, such as wars or territorial disputes, can also have a significant impact on international markets. These conflicts can disrupt supply chains, affect commodity prices, and create uncertainty about the stability of affected regions. For instance, tensions in oil-producing regions can lead to fluctuations in oil prices, affecting industries reliant on energy resources. Additionally, geopolitical conflicts can lead to capital flight, where investors seek safer assets in more stable regions, causing currency depreciation and market instability in affected areas.

Natural disasters, such as earthquakes, hurricanes, and pandemics, are another category of geopolitical events that can impact international markets. These events can cause significant economic disruptions, affecting industries such as tourism, agriculture, and manufacturing. For example, the COVID-19 pandemic led to widespread economic shutdowns, supply chain disruptions, and changes in consumer behavior, causing significant volatility in global financial markets. Understanding the potential impact of natural disasters on markets requires a comprehensive analysis of the affected regions, industries, and supply chains.

Finally, the actions of international organizations and alliances, such as the United Nations, the European Union, and the World Trade Organization, can influence global markets. These organizations play a crucial role in shaping international trade agreements, resolving disputes, and promoting economic cooperation. Their decisions and policies can have far-reaching implications for global trade, investment, and economic growth. Investors need to stay informed about the activities of these organizations to assess potential risks and opportunities in international markets.

# 4

# Chapter 4: Understanding Exchange Rates and Currency Markets

Exchange rates and currency markets play a critical role in international finance, influencing the cost of goods and services, investment returns, and economic stability. Understanding how exchange rates are determined and the factors that influence currency markets is essential for investors and businesses operating in the global economy.

Exchange rates are the value of one currency in terms of another, and they can be influenced by a variety of factors, including interest rates, inflation, and political stability. Central banks play a significant role in managing exchange rates through monetary policy and interventions in currency markets. For example, a central bank may raise interest rates to attract foreign investment and strengthen its currency, or it may intervene in the foreign exchange market by buying or selling its currency to stabilize its value.

Interest rates are a key determinant of exchange rates, as they influence the return on investments in different currencies. Higher interest rates attract foreign capital, increasing the demand for the domestic currency and causing its value to appreciate. Conversely, lower interest rates can lead to capital outflows and a depreciation of the currency. Investors closely monitor interest rate differentials between countries to identify opportunities for currency arbitrage and to manage exchange rate risk.

Inflation is another important factor that affects exchange rates. Countries with higher inflation rates tend to experience a depreciation of their currency, as the purchasing power of the currency declines relative to other currencies. Conversely, countries with low inflation rates may see their currency appreciate. Central banks use monetary policy tools, such as adjusting interest rates and controlling the money supply, to manage inflation and stabilize exchange rates.

Political stability and economic performance also play a crucial role in determining exchange rates. Countries with stable political environments and strong economic growth are more likely to attract foreign investment, leading to an appreciation of their currency. Conversely, political instability, economic downturns, and uncertainties can lead to capital flight and a depreciation of the currency. Investors need to consider the political and economic environment of countries when making decisions about currency investments.

In addition to these factors, currency markets are influenced by speculative activities and market sentiment. Traders and investors buy and sell currencies based on their expectations of future exchange rate movements, contributing to short-term fluctuations in currency values. Currency speculation can create volatility in exchange rates, requiring investors to employ risk management strategies to protect their investments.

# 5

# Chapter 5: The Role of Multinational Corporations

Multinational corporations (MNCs) play a significant role in the global economy, driving economic growth, creating jobs, and fostering innovation. These companies operate in multiple countries, leveraging their resources, expertise, and market presence to achieve competitive advantages. Understanding the strategies and challenges faced by MNCs is crucial for investors and policymakers seeking to navigate the complexities of international markets.

One of the key strategies employed by MNCs is the establishment of global supply chains. By sourcing raw materials, components, and finished products from different countries, MNCs can optimize their production processes, reduce costs, and improve efficiency. Global supply chains enable companies to take advantage of comparative advantages offered by different regions, such as lower labor costs, access to natural resources, and technological expertise. However, managing global supply chains also presents challenges, including coordination, quality control, and navigating trade regulations.

Market diversification is another important strategy for MNCs. By expanding their operations into multiple countries, companies can reduce their reliance on any single market and spread their risks. Market diversification allows MNCs to tap into new customer bases, access emerging markets, and mitigate the impact of economic downturns in specific regions. However, entering new markets requires careful analysis of local consumer preferences, regulatory environments, and competitive landscapes.

Innovation and research and development (R&D) are critical drivers of success for MNCs. These companies invest heavily in R&D to develop new products, improve existing offerings, and stay ahead of competitors. Innovation enables MNCs to differentiate themselves in the market, capture new opportunities, and drive long-term growth. Additionally, MNCs often collaborate with local research institutions, universities, and startups to harness new technologies and ideas. However, protecting intellectual property and managing R&D costs remain ongoing challenges for MNCs.

Finally, MNCs must navigate complex regulatory environments in the countries where they operate. Each country has its own set of laws and regulations governing areas such as taxation, labor practices, environmental standards, and consumer protection. Compliance with these regulations requires MNCs to invest in legal and regulatory expertise, adapt their business practices, and engage with local authorities. Failure to comply with regulations can result in fines, legal disputes, and damage to the company's reputation.

# 6

# Chapter 6: The Importance of Diversification in Investment

Diversification is a fundamental principle of investment that involves spreading investments across different asset classes, industries, and geographical regions. The primary goal of diversification is to reduce risk and improve the potential for returns. By holding a diversified portfolio, investors can mitigate the impact of poor performance in any single investment and increase the likelihood of achieving positive overall returns.

One of the key benefits of diversification is the reduction of unsystematic risk, which is the risk associated with individual investments. For example, if an investor holds stocks in multiple companies across different industries, the poor performance of one company is less likely to significantly impact the overall portfolio. Diversification helps smooth out the volatility of returns and provides a more stable investment experience.

Geographical diversification is another important aspect of investment strategy. By investing in different countries and regions, investors can take advantage of varying economic conditions, growth opportunities, and currency movements. Geographical diversification also helps protect against country-specific risks, such as political instability, economic downturns, and natural disasters. For example, while the economy of one country may be experiencing a recession, another country may be enjoying robust growth, offsetting the negative impact on the overall portfolio.

Diversification across asset classes is also crucial for managing risk. Different asset classes, such as stocks, bonds, real estate, and commodities, have varying risk and return characteristics. By holding a mix of asset classes, investors can balance the risk and potential returns of their portfolio. For example, while stocks may offer higher returns, they also come with higher volatility. Bonds, on the other hand, provide more stable returns but with lower growth potential. A diversified portfolio that includes both stocks and bonds can provide a balance between growth and stability.

Finally, sector diversification involves spreading investments across different industries. This strategy helps protect against sector-specific risks, such as technological disruptions, regulatory changes, and shifts in consumer preferences. For example, an investor who holds stocks in the technology, healthcare, and energy sectors can benefit from the growth potential of each industry while mitigating the impact of challenges faced by any single sector.

# 7

# Chapter 7: Risk Management in International Investments

Risk management is a critical aspect of international investments, as investors must navigate a range of risks that can impact their returns and overall portfolio performance. These risks include currency risk, political risk, economic risk, and market risk. Developing effective risk management strategies is essential for protecting investments and achieving long-term financial goals.

Currency risk, also known as exchange rate risk, arises from fluctuations in the value of currencies. When investors hold assets denominated in foreign currencies, changes in exchange rates can affect the value of their investments. For example, if an investor holds stocks in a European company and the euro depreciates against the investor's home currency, the value of the investment will decline. To manage currency risk, investors can use hedging strategies such as forward contracts, options, and currency swaps to lock in exchange rates and reduce exposure to currency fluctuations.

Political risk is the risk associated with changes in government policies, political instability, and geopolitical events. These factors can impact the investment climate and the performance of assets in a particular country. For example, changes in trade policies, taxation, and regulations can affect the profitability of investments. To mitigate political risk, investors can diversify their investments across multiple countries and regions, conduct thorough due diligence on the political environment, and engage with local stakeholders to understand potential risks and opportunities.

Economic risk is related to the overall economic conditions of a country or region. Factors such as inflation, interest rates, economic growth, and unemployment can impact the performance of investments. For example, high inflation can erode the purchasing power of returns, while economic recessions can lead to declines in asset values. To manage economic risk, investors can diversify their portfolios across different asset classes, industries, and geographical regions. Additionally, staying informed about macroeconomic trends and indicators can help investors make informed decisions and adjust their strategies accordingly.

Market risk, also known as systematic risk, is the risk associated with the overall performance of financial markets. Factors such as market volatility, investor sentiment, and global economic conditions can affect the value of investments. To manage market risk, investors can employ strategies such as asset allocation, diversification, and regular portfolio rebalancing. By holding a mix of asset classes and regularly reviewing their portfolio, investors can reduce exposure to market fluctuations and achieve a more balanced risk-return profile.

# 8

# Chapter 8: The Role of Technology in Global Finance

Technology has revolutionized the world of global finance, transforming how financial transactions are conducted, data is analyzed, and investment decisions are made. The rapid advancement of technology has led to the development of new financial instruments, platforms, and services that have reshaped the landscape of international markets.

One of the most significant technological advancements in global finance is the rise of financial technology, or fintech. Fintech encompasses a wide range of innovations, including digital payments, online lending platforms, robo-advisors, and blockchain technology. These innovations have made financial services more accessible, efficient, and cost-effective. For example, digital payment platforms such as PayPal and mobile banking apps have simplified the process of transferring money across borders, reducing transaction costs and increasing convenience for consumers and businesses.

Data analytics and artificial intelligence (AI) have also had a profound impact on global finance. The ability to collect, analyze, and interpret vast amounts of data has enabled financial institutions to gain deeper insights into market trends, customer behavior, and risk factors. AI-powered algorithms can analyze complex data sets in real-time, providing valuable information for investment decisions, risk management, and regulatory compliance. For example, machine learning algorithms can identify patterns in financial markets, helping investors make more informed trading decisions.

Blockchain technology has the potential to revolutionize international finance by providing a secure, transparent, and efficient way to conduct transactions. Blockchain is a decentralized ledger technology that allows for the recording and verification of transactions without the need for intermediaries. This technology can reduce transaction costs, increase transparency, and enhance security in areas such as cross-border payments, supply chain management, and asset tokenization. For example, blockchain-based platforms such as Ripple and Ethereum are being used to facilitate international payments and smart contracts.

The rise of digital currencies, such as Bitcoin and other cryptocurrencies, has also transformed the global financial landscape. Digital currencies offer an alternative to traditional fiat currencies, providing new opportunities for investment, payment, and financial inclusion. However, the volatility and regulatory challenges associated with digital currencies pose risks that investors need to consider. Understanding the technology, regulatory environment, and potential use cases of digital currencies is essential for navigating this emerging asset class.

# 9

# Chapter 9: The Influence of Global Trade Agreements

Global trade agreements play a crucial role in shaping the landscape of international markets and investments. These agreements are negotiated between countries to facilitate trade by reducing tariffs, eliminating trade barriers, and promoting economic cooperation. Understanding the impact of global trade agreements is essential for investors and businesses seeking to navigate the complexities of international trade.

One of the most significant global trade agreements is the World Trade Organization (WTO) agreements. The WTO is an international organization that oversees global trade rules and promotes fair and open trade among member countries. The WTO agreements cover a wide range of trade-related issues, including goods, services, intellectual property, and dispute resolution. By providing a framework for trade negotiations and resolving trade disputes, the WTO helps create a stable and predictable trading environment, benefiting businesses and investors.

Regional trade agreements, such as the North American Free Trade Agreement (NAFTA) and its successor, the United States-Mexico-Canada Agreement (USMCA), have also had a significant impact on international trade. These agreements aim to eliminate tariffs and reduce trade barriers among member countries, fostering economic integration and increasing market access. For example, NAFTA eliminated tariffs on most goods traded between the United States, Canada, and Mexico, leading to increased trade and investment flows among the three countries. The USMCA builds on NAFTA's foundation, incorporating new provisions on labor rights, environmental standards, and digital trade.

Another important regional trade agreement is the European Union (EU) Single Market. The Single Market allows for the free movement of goods, services, capital, and people among EU member states, creating a unified economic area. This integration has facilitated cross-border trade and investment, providing businesses with access to a large and diverse market. The Single Market also promotes regulatory harmonization, reducing compliance costs and simplifying trade procedures for businesses operating in the EU.

The Comprehensive and Progressive Agreement for Trans-Pacific Partnership (CPTPP) is another significant trade agreement that includes countries from Asia, the Americas, and Oceania. The CPTPP aims to reduce tariffs and non-tariff barriers, promote trade in goods and services, and enhance economic cooperation among member countries. The agreement covers a wide range of issues, including intellectual property, labor standards, and environmental protection. By providing new market opportunities and strengthening economic ties, the CPTPP has the potential to boost trade and investment in the Asia-Pacific region.

# 10

# Chapter 10: The Future of International Markets

The future of international markets is shaped by a range of factors, including technological advancements, demographic changes, geopolitical developments, and environmental challenges. Understanding these trends and their potential impact on global markets is essential for investors and businesses seeking to navigate the evolving landscape of international finance.

Technological advancements, such as artificial intelligence, blockchain, and digital currencies, are expected to continue transforming international markets. These technologies have the potential to increase efficiency, reduce transaction costs, and create new opportunities for innovation and growth. For example, AI-powered algorithms can enhance investment strategies by analyzing large data sets and identifying patterns in financial markets. Blockchain technology can improve transparency and security shaping the future of global finance, while digital currencies may create new avenues for investment and financial inclusion. However, these technologies also pose challenges, including regulatory concerns, cybersecurity risks, and the potential for market disruption.

Demographic changes, such as aging populations and urbanization, will also influence the future of international markets. Aging populations in developed countries may lead to shifts in consumer demand, labor force participation, and government spending on healthcare and pensions. Urbanization in emerging markets can drive economic growth, create new business opportunities, and increase demand for infrastructure, housing, and services. Understanding these demographic trends is essential for identifying investment opportunities and managing risks in international markets.

Geopolitical developments, such as changes in trade policies, regional conflicts, and shifts in global power dynamics, will continue to impact international markets. The rise of emerging economies, such as China and India, will reshape the global economic landscape, creating new opportunities for trade and investment. However, geopolitical tensions and protectionist policies can disrupt global supply chains, affect market stability, and create uncertainty for investors. Staying informed about geopolitical developments and their potential impact on international markets is crucial for making informed investment decisions.

Environmental challenges, such as climate change and resource scarcity, will also play a significant role in shaping the future of international markets. The transition to a low-carbon economy, the increasing demand for renewable energy, and the need for sustainable resource management will create new opportunities and risks for businesses and investors. Companies that adopt sustainable practices and invest in green technologies may benefit from regulatory incentives, consumer preferences, and long-term cost savings. However, businesses that fail to address environmental challenges may face regulatory penalties, reputational risks, and increased costs.

# 11

# Chapter 11: Emerging Markets and Investment Opportunities

Emerging markets present significant investment opportunities for investors seeking higher returns and diversification. These markets, characterized by rapid economic growth, expanding middle classes, and increasing integration into the global economy, offer a range of opportunities across different sectors and asset classes.

One of the key drivers of investment opportunities in emerging markets is economic growth. Many emerging economies, such as China, India, and Brazil, have experienced substantial economic growth over the past few decades, driven by factors such as industrialization, urbanization, and rising consumer spending. This growth has created opportunities for businesses and investors in industries such as manufacturing, technology, and consumer goods. However, investing in emerging markets also comes with risks, including political instability, regulatory challenges, and currency fluctuations.

The expanding middle class in emerging markets is another important factor creating investment opportunities. As incomes rise and living standards improve, there is increasing demand for a wide range of goods and services, including healthcare, education, housing, and entertainment. Companies that cater to the needs and preferences of the emerging middle class can benefit from strong consumer demand and market growth. For example, the growth of e-commerce and digital payments in emerging markets has created opportunities for technology companies and financial services providers.

Infrastructure development is also a key area of investment in emerging markets. Many emerging economies are investing in infrastructure projects, such as transportation, energy, and telecommunications, to support economic growth and improve living standards. These projects create opportunities for businesses in construction, engineering, and related industries. Additionally, infrastructure development can enhance connectivity and accessibility, facilitating trade and investment flows between regions.

Financial markets in emerging economies are becoming more sophisticated and accessible, providing new opportunities for investment. Stock exchanges, bond markets, and private equity funds in emerging markets offer a range of investment options for domestic and international investors. For example, the growth of stock exchanges in countries such as India and Brazil has provided opportunities for investors to gain exposure to high-growth companies and industries. Additionally, the development of financial markets can improve access to capital for businesses, supporting economic growth and innovation.

# 12

# Chapter 12: Strategies for Successful International Investing

Successful international investing requires a combination of thorough research, strategic planning, and risk management. Investors need to understand the unique characteristics of international markets, identify opportunities, and develop strategies to achieve their financial goals while managing risks.

One of the key strategies for successful international investing is conducting thorough research and due diligence. Investors should analyze the economic, political, and regulatory environment of the countries where they plan to invest. This includes assessing factors such as GDP growth, inflation rates, interest rates, trade policies, and political stability. Additionally, investors should conduct detailed analysis of the industries and companies they are considering, examining factors such as competitive positioning, financial performance, and growth prospects. Thorough research helps investors make informed decisions and identify potential risks and opportunities.

Diversification is another important strategy for international investing. By spreading investments across different countries, regions, and asset classes, investors can reduce the impact of poor performance in any single market or investment. Diversification helps manage risks and increase the potential for positive returns. For example, investors can diversify their portfolio by investing in a mix of developed and emerging markets, different industries, and various asset classes such as stocks, bonds, and real estate.

Currency risk management is also crucial for international investing. Fluctuations in exchange rates can impact the value of investments and returns. Investors can use hedging strategies such as forward contracts, options, and currency swaps to protect against adverse currency movements. Additionally, investors should consider the impact of currency risk on their overall portfolio and adjust their investment strategies accordingly. For example, investing in local currency-denominated assets or using currency-hedged funds can help manage currency risk.

Staying informed about global economic and market trends is essential for successful international investing. Investors should monitor developments in international markets, such as changes in trade policies, geopolitical events, and economic indicators. Staying informed helps investors anticipate potential risks and opportunities and make timely adjustments to their investment strategies. Additionally, investors should consider the impact of macroeconomic trends, such as technological advancements, demographic changes, and environmental challenges, on their investments.

Finally, investors should develop a long-term investment strategy that aligns with their financial goals and risk tolerance. International investing can be complex and volatile, and it requires a disciplined approach. Investors should set clear objectives, establish a diversified portfolio, and regularly review and adjust their investment strategy. A long-term perspective helps investors navigate short-term market fluctuations and stay focused on achieving their financial goals.

# 13

# Chapter 13: The Role of Ethical and Sustainable Investing

Ethical and sustainable investing has gained increasing prominence in the world of international finance. Investors are increasingly considering environmental, social, and governance (ESG) factors when making investment decisions, seeking to generate positive social and environmental impact alongside financial returns. Understanding the principles and practices of ethical and sustainable investing is essential for investors looking to align their investments with their values.

One of the key principles of ethical investing is the consideration of ESG factors in investment analysis and decision-making. Environmental factors include issues such as climate change, resource management, and pollution. Social factors encompass areas such as labor practices, human rights, and community impact. Governance factors involve corporate governance practices, such as board diversity, executive compensation, and transparency. By integrating ESG factors into their investment process, investors can identify companies that are well-positioned to manage risks and capitalize on opportunities related to sustainability.

Sustainable investing involves investing in companies and projects that contribute to sustainable development goals, such as clean energy, affordable healthcare, and access to education. This approach aims to address global challenges such as climate change, poverty, and inequality while generating financial returns. For example, investing in renewable energy projects, such as solar and wind power, can contribute to reducing carbon emissions and promoting energy security. Similarly, investing in companies that provide access to clean water and sanitation can improve public health and quality of life.

Impact investing is a subset of sustainable investing that focuses on generating measurable social and environmental impact alongside financial returns. Impact investors seek to create positive change in areas such as healthcare, education, and economic development. For example, investing in microfinance institutions can provide access to financial services for underserved populations, promoting financial inclusion and economic empowerment. Impact investing requires a rigorous approach to measuring and reporting the social and environmental outcomes of investments.

Ethical and sustainable investing also involves active ownership and engagement with companies. Investors can use their influence as shareholders to advocate for improved ESG practices and promote corporate accountability. This includes voting on shareholder resolutions, engaging in dialogue with company management, and collaborating with other investors to drive positive change. Active ownership helps investors align their investments with their values and contribute to a more sustainable and equitable global economy.

# 14

# Chapter 14: The Role of Financial Institutions in Global Markets

Financial institutions play a crucial role in the functioning of global markets, providing the infrastructure, services, and capital needed to facilitate economic activity and investment. Understanding the different types of financial institutions and their roles in international markets is essential for investors and businesses.

Commercial banks are one of the primary types of financial institutions, providing a range of services such as deposit-taking, lending, and payment processing. Commercial banks facilitate the flow of capital by offering loans to individuals, businesses, and governments, enabling investment and economic growth. They also provide payment services, such as wire transfers and electronic payments, that facilitate international trade and transactions. Additionally, commercial banks offer foreign exchange services, helping clients manage currency risk and conduct cross-border transactions.

Investment banks specialize in providing capital markets services, such as underwriting, mergers and acquisitions (M&A), and trading. Investment banks help companies raise capital by issuing stocks and bonds, enabling them to finance expansion and investment projects. They also provide advisory services for M&A transactions, helping companies navigate complex deals and achieve strategic objectives. Investment banks play a key role in the functioning of financial markets by facilitating the buying and selling of securities, providing liquidity, and helping clients manage risk.

Asset management firms manage investment portfolios on behalf of individuals, institutions, and governments. These firms offer a range of investment products, such as mutual funds, exchange-traded funds (ETFs), and private equity funds, that provide exposure to different asset classes and investment strategies. Asset managers conduct research and analysis to identify investment opportunities, allocate capital, and manage risk. They play a critical role in channeling capital to productive investments, supporting economic growth and innovation.

Pension funds and insurance companies are institutional investors that manage large pools of capital to meet the future financial obligations of their beneficiaries and policyholders. Pension funds invest in a diverse range of assets, including stocks, bonds, real estate, and alternative investments, to generate returns that will fund retirement benefits. Insurance companies, on the other hand, invest premiums collected from policyholders to pay for future claims. Both pension funds and insurance companies play a significant role in the global financial markets, providing stability and long-term capital for investments.

Sovereign wealth funds are state-owned investment funds that manage a portion of a country's reserves to achieve long-term financial objectives. These funds invest in a wide range of assets, including equities, bonds, real estate, and infrastructure projects, to generate returns and diversify the country's revenue sources. Sovereign wealth funds play a crucial role in global markets by providing significant capital for investments and contributing to economic development.

# 15

# Chapter 15: The Path Forward for Global Investors

As global markets continue to evolve, investors must remain agile and forward-thinking to navigate the complexities and capitalize on emerging opportunities. The path forward for global investors involves embracing technological advancements, staying informed about global trends, and adopting strategies that align with long-term financial goals.

Technological advancements, such as artificial intelligence, blockchain, and digital currencies, will continue to shape the future of international markets. Investors should stay abreast of these developments and consider how they can leverage new technologies to enhance their investment strategies. For example, AI-powered analytics can provide valuable insights into market trends, while blockchain technology can improve the transparency and efficiency of financial transactions. Embracing technology will enable investors to stay competitive and make informed decisions in an increasingly digital world.

Staying informed about global trends is essential for identifying opportunities and managing risks in international markets. Investors should monitor economic indicators, geopolitical developments, and regulatory changes that may impact their investments. Additionally, understanding demographic shifts, environmental challenges, and technological disruptions will help investors anticipate potential risks and opportunities. Staying informed requires a proactive approach to research, continuous learning, and engagement with industry experts and thought leaders.

Adopting a long-term investment strategy is crucial for navigating the uncertainties of international markets. A disciplined approach to investing, based on thorough research, diversification, and risk management, will help investors achieve their financial goals. Investors should set clear objectives, establish a diversified portfolio, and regularly review and adjust their investment strategies. A long-term perspective will enable investors to weather short-term market fluctuations and stay focused on achieving sustainable returns.

Finally, investors should consider the principles of ethical and sustainable investing as they navigate the complexities of global markets. Integrating environmental, social, and governance (ESG) factors into investment decisions can create positive social and environmental impact alongside financial returns. Ethical and sustainable investing aligns investments with values and contributes to a more equitable and sustainable global economy. By considering the broader impact of their investments, investors can play a role in addressing global challenges and driving positive change.

In conclusion, the journey through international markets and investments is a complex and dynamic odyssey. By understanding the foundation of international markets, the role of central banks, the impact of geopolitical events, and the importance of diversification and risk management, investors can navigate the complexities and seize opportunities. Embracing technology, staying informed about global trends, adopting a long-term investment strategy, and considering ethical and sustainable investing principles will empower investors to achieve their financial goals and contribute to a more prosperous and sustainable future.

**Financial Odyssey: Navigating the Complexities of International Markets and Investments**

Embark on an enlightening journey through the intricate world of international finance with "Financial Odyssey: Navigating the Complexities of

## CHAPTER 15: THE PATH FORWARD FOR GLOBAL INVESTORS

International Markets and Investments." This comprehensive guide demystifies the labyrinth of global markets, offering readers a deep understanding of how international trade, currency fluctuations, and geopolitical events shape the financial landscape.

Each of the 15 expertly crafted chapters delves into crucial topics, from the foundational principles of international markets and the pivotal role of central banks to the impact of geopolitical events and the rise of technology in finance. Discover the strategies employed by multinational corporations, the importance of diversification in investment, and the essential risk management techniques for navigating the unpredictable waters of global finance.

Whether you're an aspiring investor, a seasoned professional, or simply curious about the forces that drive the global economy, this book provides valuable insights and practical knowledge. Learn how to harness emerging market opportunities, manage ethical and sustainable investments, and leverage technological advancements to stay ahead in an ever-evolving financial world.

"Financial Odyssey" is your indispensable companion for understanding and thriving in the complex realm of international markets and investments. Join us on this odyssey and unlock the secrets to achieving financial success on a global scale.

www.ingramcontent.com/pod-product-compliance
Lightning Source LLC
LaVergne TN
LVHW020502080526
838202LV00057B/6100